Time Management

Optimizing Productivity And Achieving Achievement With The Implementation Of Efficient Morning Time Management Techniques

(Foundational Time Management Skills For Novices)

MarcinZysk

TABLE OF CONTENT

Introduction 1

Managing Time at Work 19

Beating Time Wasters and Taking Charge of Your Time 24

How to Evaluate and Enhance the Performance of Your Team 41

Successful Guidance 62

How do productivity and time management relate to each other? 81

Recognising time wasters and put off tasks 101

Beyond the Pill: Using Medication and Therapy Together for Efficient Time Management) 116

If you put things off for too long, you'll miss out on enjoyable experiences 144

Introduction

We all have a finite amount of time each day, making it valuable. Manage our time well. Whether you're a professional, a mother, a student, or an entrepreneur, managing your time well can help you reach your objectives and increase your output.

The primary ideas of time management—prioritization, organizational structure, efficiency, procrastination, work-life balance, multitasking, task delegation, time blocking, meeting management, deadline management, distraction control, time-saving strategies, focus and concentration, time auditing, and time tracking—will all be covered in this book.

After reading this book, you will have a firm grasp of the best time management methods and approaches you may use daily. You'll have improved time management skills, be able to focus on what needs to be done more quickly and reduce distractions. Come on, let's get started!

He or she knows that if they do anything wrong, they will lose respect from society and items that are worth money. To punish every individual in society would be to discipline it. A society that lacks discipline will see an increase in immorality and abuse. Under such circumstances, it will be difficult to maintain.

If people don't consider the consequences, they will act however they like, causing chaos and disturbance. Consequently, laws and regulations must be put in place to protect such situations. It will be essential to lead by example and to punish offenders. This is the only way society can move closer to harmony and peace.

If communal discipline is upheld, an individual within a society can have a peaceful and respectful life. It prevents significant societal problems by upholding law and order. To function well, society may need to be disciplined.

Discipline flourishes in such a society, but everyone is treated unfairly.

Something has to be constant and uniform to be successful.

While a disciplined approach might succeed, a disorganized and haphazard one might not and require many more resources. As they say, discipline is essential to life.

In conclusion

Discipline is important because it is important on two levels: personally and in terms of society structure. Developing mental habits that encourage conscious thinking among other members of society is advantageous.

His mental state reveals his personality and point of view. It requires mental and physical discipline. The enemy of both is discipline, which forces them to concentrate more closely on their objectives.

A person's physical and mental health may deteriorate with anxiety and depression.

Discipline combined with emotional restraint can help with these kinds of problems. Discipline appears to deal with personal issues thus far.

Remember that consistency is important for more than just reaching objectives; it helps with relationship maintenance, trust and loyalty building, and being dependable. Consistency in our actions, attitudes, and choices throughout life establishes our credibility, and people are drawn to persons who exhibit consistency.

In conclusion, consistency is an effective instrument for accomplishing our objectives and fulfilling lives. We should all try to live up to it in all we do since it is the secret to success. Generations to come will be inspired by Jack's story, which serves as a reminder of the value of consistency.

Self-awareness and discipline go hand in hand. We can learn to identify unhealthy patterns in our thinking and behavior and make necessary changes before they have detrimental effects by increasing our awareness of these aspects of ourselves. Being self-aware also enables us to recognize the situations and people that set off our impulsive behavior and to devise countermeasures.

Formulating a strategy: After establishing your objectives, creating a plan that details the precise actions you'll take to get them is critical. Setting deadlines, determining the resources you'll need, and dividing more complex objectives into smaller, more doable tasks are all part of this process.

Any goal or target must be achieved by first creating an action plan. A well-thought-out plan of action can boost your chances of success and help you keep focused and organized, whether you're an individual. The main components of an action plan and techniques for making and carrying out a plan are as follows:

Establishing a precise aim or target is the first stage in creating an action plan. Despite its apparent simplicity, this is frequently the most challenging step in planning. Try to be as specific as you can while stating your objective. For example, consider saying, "I want to lose 10 pounds in the next six months," rather than, "I want to lose weight." After you have a specific objective, you may start breaking it into more manageable, smaller steps.

Making a timeline is the next stage in coming up with a strategy. A timeline is a graphic depiction of your plan that aids in understanding the stages you must take to reach your objective and helps you see the big picture. Deadlines for each phase and milestones—important moments in the process that show progress—should be included on a timetable. Goal and stay on course by doing this.

Chapter 3: Modern World Time Management Techniques

Effective time management is more important than ever in the fast-paced world of the twenty-first century, where time frequently seems to be a finite resource. To become a time management virtuoso, you must first comprehend the value of time, set meaningful goals, and overcome procrastination, as you have seen in the previous chapters. Now, let's explore the methods and approaches enabling you to prosper in the modern environment. Remember that although time may be passing quickly, these tactics are meant to ensure you don't get left behind!

How technology may help with time management
The Predicament of Digital Getting Around in the Age of Distractions
The capacity to focus and avoid distractions is a daily struggle for many of us in a world where social media, cell phones, and constant notifications rule the roost.

Imagine you're working on a task when your phone suddenly alerts you to something, and you become distracted by the unending social media scroll. Does this sound familiar? You are not by yourself. The digital problem presents a significant difficulty today, but the good news is that you have control over it.

Realistic Methods for Taking Back Control

Mastering Alerts: Notifications on your phone sound like a colorful parade—buzzing, beeping, and flashing. However, do you need to answer every ping? Inhale deeply and explore your notification preferences. It's possible to focus for short periods by turning off unnecessary alarms.

Setting Up Areas Without Devices: Do you recall when family meals were sacrosanct occasions that weren't affected by screens? Establishing device-free areas, such as your bedroom or dining table, will help you reclaim that feeling of community. Make these areas a refuge for sincere discussions and relaxation.

Using Applications for Productivity: Technology can be a distraction, but it can also be the key to more effective time management. Apps for productivity, such as time trackers and task managers, can be your dependable allies. You can remain focused and maximize every moment with the aid of these digital assistants.

Conscientious Web Surfing: The internet may be a time-consuming maze that leads you into rabbit holes while providing fun and knowledge. Set a timer for your online activity to engage in mindful browsing. Once the timer goes off, end the cat videos and complete your to-do list.

Recall the Digital Environment.

The digital world presents countless opportunities, but you must manage it purposefully. You lead your digital experience. You'll overcome the digital problem with a renewed sense of time management if you learn to regulate digital distractions and leverage technology to your benefit.

Effectiveness and Efficiency: Finding a Balance

In time management, efficacy and efficiency are two sides of the same coin. Effectiveness ensures you're doing the proper things, while efficiency gets things done faster. This section will cover how to combine these two factors to increase your output without compromising the caliber of your work.

The Efficiency Dilemma

Envision a bustling beehive where workers are zipping about at an unequaled speed, finishing each assignment in record time. This is efficiency in action, a rapid-fire symphony of movements. The catch is that quality isn't always ensured by efficiency alone. Although you may easily cross things off your to-do list, are they helping you achieve your ultimate objectives?

The Mysteries of Effectiveness

Imagine that a master painter painstakingly and precisely creates each brushstroke. This is the art of effectiveness: producing significant and influential work. It could take longer to get right, but the quality is evident. Take caution, though, as pursuing perfection could slow you down and accumulate unfinished jobs.

Finding the Balance

Thus, how does the tango balance between efficacy and efficiency? This is the secret sauce: order everything according to importance and urgency. It's similar to leading an orchestra by focusing your efforts where they are most needed. You're not simply accomplishing tasks but moving closer to your long-term objectives when you give your actions meaning.

Productivity Maximisation Without Quality Sacrifice

Set Purpose-driven Priorities: Every task is not made equal. Determine which of your goals are high-impact, high-urgency tasks to focus on. These are the things that you should prioritize most.

Aim to deliver quality while keeping a constant pace and approach them with a balanced perspective.

Blocking Time: Consider each day's time blocks as a canvas. You may create an organized environment that promotes productivity without sacrificing quality by allocating certain blocks to different tasks. Making each note contribute to the final product is like creating a symphony of labor.

Combining related tasks in one batch: Your workflow can be streamlined by combining related jobs into groups. You're in the zone, maximizing your productivity without overcommitting yourself instead of hopping between different jobs.

Managing Time at Work

The value of time management in the workplace

Successful and productive time management is essential for success in the workplace.

This chapter will cover methods and approaches for increasing productivity and making the most use of your time at work.

Setting Priorities

Establishing your priorities is a crucial first step in time management at work.

Here are some pointers to assist you:

Evaluate the tasks:

Examine your tasks and decide which are most essential and crucial.

Give these chores top priority and provide enough time to finish them.

Establish Daily Objectives: Establish specific daily objectives to direct your work efforts.

You'll be able to maintain focus and concentrate your efforts on the things that count.

Time-Management Strategies in the Workplace

You can use several efficient time management strategies in the office.

These are a handful of the most well-liked ones:

The Pomodoro Method: Employ the Pomodoro approach, which has you working in concentrated intervals—

typically 25 minutes—interspersed with quick breaks for recovery.

This method aids in preserving focus and preventing fatigue.

Assigning work that other team members can complete is a good idea.

By doing this, you may divide the workload and concentrate on more important things.

Email management: Instead of being interrupted by emails all the time, set up specific times to check and reply to them.

Use folders or tags to organize your email to maintain a more productive workflow.

Steer clear of excessive multitasking: Attempting to accomplish too many tasks at once may be appealing, but doing so frequently leads to decreased productivity.

Concentrate on one activity at a time, finishing it before going on to the next.

Removing Diversions

Distractions at work have the potential to seriously impair time management.

Here are some strategies to reduce distractions and boost productivity:

Disable Notifications: Disable notifications from mobile apps and devices that can interfere with your work.

This will allow you to work on projects without being constantly distracted.

Establish a Focused Workplace: Set up your workspace to reduce outside distractions.

Keep your space neat and orderly, and eliminate anything extra that could divert your attention.

Establish Time Restrictions for Talks and Interruptions: Use assertiveness when establishing time restrictions for social interactions and talks at work.

This keeps you from getting sidetracked and demonstrates to coworkers that you are committed to your work.

Beating Time Wasters and Taking Charge of Your Time

It is normal for us to have times when we waste time. For instance, while pursuing my bachelor's degree, I became proficient at a piano roll rhythm game I would play in my spare time. For the others, this may have been a perfect diversion. But as I played the game more and more, I found that I was spending so much time on it that I would frequently put off doing things that would be more beneficial. Luckily, the game's support was finally withdrawn, allowing me to resume my progress. It took me a week or two to realize that time wasn't hollow despite the habit of being torn from me. We'll discuss a few ineffective endeavors that belong in the fourth quadrant of your Eisenhower Matrix. Put differently, they are chores that don't bring value to your life and are best left undone.

Recognizing and Breaking Time-Wasteful Habits

Time-wasting pursuits frequently elude us. They might not seem like much at first, but once we get involved, we'll discover that we needed those forty-five minutes we spent scrolling through photos of our coworker's pet to move the project along. I'll enumerate some typical time wasters. I'd like you to take a moment to reflect before I move on. Consider the things you've done at work without giving them any attention. Which one of these produced results? Which one was not? Was there anything you could have done to prevent interacting with folks who negatively affected your productivity in the first place?

It's possible that pointless meetings were on your mind. Thankfully, you can help colleagues on diverse teams by imparting your enhanced knowledge when they are appropriate. Anxiety is a less spoken, but possibly even more prevalent, time waster. It's normal to have some nervousness when faced with a problem. I'm referring to the kind where we frequently divide our attention due to confusing instructions or a desire to multitask. Consequently, the caliber of the job we produce suffers. If the outcomes were insufficient, we frequently overestimate the time needed to complete the task. Box breathing is what I suggest to help with this problem. It's a very easy strategy that works well under time constraints. Inhale deeply. Hold your breath in your lungs and slowly count backward from one to four. Next, release the breath. Breathe in after once more, counting to four. Rinse, then carry out this procedure as often as necessary. I like to close my eyes when box breathing because it helps me feel more connected to my body.

Working on completely unrelated tasks during work hours is another major waste of time. Even worse, most of these don't compromise productivity in favor of an alternative long-term gain. Rather, most of us have battled with spending several hours on Reddit to get kicks or engaging in gossip about various circles in our lives. Approximately 50% of workers send messages during work more frequently than they believe is appropriate. They gossip while they know there are more important chores to complete, which is an excellent third report. There is no reason to feel bad about these numbers. Rather, engage in attentive meditation. Admit that there have been times when you have misallocated your time, and instead of punishing yourself, put a plan in place to reduce these distractions.

Now that we know some typical sources of distraction, let's examine strategies for avoiding them. One of my favorite tactics is from a physician I like to call Dr. K. Kanojia, who takes us through the scenario of a client who had trouble focusing on a little video essay. This man would eventually give in on tasks that weren't urgent or even that necessary because he thought he was wasting his time otherwise. Within this perspective, Kanojia explains why the mind wanders. Our brains aren't built to handle idleness and inaction. Yet, they frequently lack the motivation to devote their energies to pressing responsibilities. He suggests using a method his father taught him to fix this. It involves narrowing down your selections and focusing on your project. You have three options: work, sleep, or wait until it feels right to work. Other activities are not permitted. Because of this constraint, your brain is practically forced to "play chicken" with you. If you practice willpower, you will ultimately discover that working is the least resistance.

A more focused approach would be to intentionally use the Pomodoro technique. As Pomodoros are naturally inseparable, assign a particular number to the current task. It can be difficult to deal with possible restarts until you get used to them, but it will eventually get easier. It is more productive to actively try to avoid distractions than simply letting the mind wander whenever it pleases. Engaging in activities like meditation naturally heightens our awareness of our environment and the present moment. Help yourself with the resources from earlier in the book, which enhance the analysis we've done here.

Maintaining awareness can differ slightly from making quick corrections. But it is predicated on concepts we examined over this time management trip. For example, developing self-awareness makes recognizing when we've adopted a new time-wasting habit easier. Most of the time, you can break the wasteful pattern before it becomes ingrained in your life. Being alert is usually sufficient to weed out the most frequent and occasionally uncommon time wasters.

As insurance, whenever you check your goals and plan, consider whether you've lately squandered time. Don't condemn yourself when you respond; just be honest. Problems do not characterize a person as evil. It makes them more human. We can identify with imperfect media figures. Compared to someone with a great life, their situation feels more genuine. But we must work at it if we want the metaphor to make sense. Start with your own life story, please. And strive to succeed despite your obstacles. Rather than just drifting, overcome. To do this, it is wise to examine how we make decisions. Although each person's process is unique, we may frequently rely on tools to help us adjust. So, let's assess a few concepts that can help us become better problem solvers.

Every plan requires defense.

How to Keep Your Plan Safe

Why would you allow someone to ruin a plan you spent hours constructing out of respect for your time and yourself?

Learning to value your time is the first step in safeguarding your strategy. You live in the now. Your money is your prime time.

Prevent Interruptions: Don't answer if your plan calls for specific times during the day. If you must answer these calls, restrict the number using caller ID or staff screening. When using your computer, avoid allowing email pop-ups to appear. (More about disruptions in the upcoming chapter.)

Plan Your Reactive Activities: Make slots during the day for when you will answer phones, read and reply to emails, and tolerate interruptions!

A backup plan could be one of the most effective ways to save time. No matter how well you prepare, uncontrollable events or occurrences will happen and give you unexpected time. An employee may be late, your appointment won't happen, or you'll have to wait for one. Use useful things as a backup plan in case something goes wrong.

Maintain Meeting Times: Ensure that meetings begin on time and end on schedule, paying equal attention to both. Observe the agenda for meetings.

Be Ready: Allocate time in your schedule to get ready for the following task.

Be Realistic: Try to estimate the time you set aside for each task as precisely as possible.

Break Yourself In Although most small business owners have high hopes and are hopeful, start out slowly if you are not accustomed to a schedule. During the day, give yourself permission to take breaks and reflect.

Collaborate as a Team and Tell Others - Inform coworkers, clients, vendors, employees, and other colleagues that you will adhere to a new schedule. It may surprise you how many people are willing to assist you in safeguarding your plan.

Establish Expectations:

Teach them what to expect from you.

Inform them that business is done with a sense of urgency.

Arrive early, arrive on time for appointments and meetings, get to the point, wrap up, and depart on time.

Show others courtesy. It is impolite to arrive late or to keep others waiting. It is rude to disregard other people's time. The essence of existence is time. It does not demonstrate your importance to keep people waiting for meetings and appointments. It demonstrates your rudeness. You should first respect other people's time if you want them to respect yours.

Be Kind and Allocate Particular Time for Others. Indicate to people regularly when you are available for spontaneous meetings or chats. Individuals accustomed to "popping in" during your day and occasionally having crucial information will still get in touch with you, particularly if they know that they will have a designated time slot. Give them time to become used to your timetable while remaining firm. (This does not imply that you should give in to inefficient use of your time.)

Blame the clock! It is sufficient to say something like, "The clock says I have to go now," or "According to the clock, I have to get to my next meeting," when someone has reached the end of their appointment or time slot. Since it's difficult to argue with a clock, most people won't protest to you getting off the hook for doing this!

You can set goals to eliminate your time wasters once you've assessed where your time is spent. Make use of organizing tools to assist you in reaching your objectives. A day planner, software like Microsoft Outlook, or a Palm Pilot can be your first choice. Sort the daily duties according to priority, using whichever method you prefer. Establish your short- and long-term deadlines and the tasks that must be completed now and in the future.

This list should be reviewed as needed. Make time on your agenda for unforeseen events at all times. You should dedicate twenty to thirty hours a week to particular duties. Nonetheless, try to budget around ten hours for unforeseen events. You never know when a personal issue can arise and require attention or when you'll need to devote more time than you anticipated to a project.

7. The Value of Reporting and Tracking Time.

How to Evaluate and Enhance the Performance of Your Team

In this chapter, we'll look at the value of time tracking and reporting in leading an effective team. We'll go over the advantages of time monitoring, how to set it up, and how to use the information you gather from time tracking to maximize team productivity.

1. The Value of Time Monitoring

Time tracking is crucial for assessing your team's output and pinpointing areas needing development. You can determine which tasks consume the most time by keeping track of the time spent on them and modifying your workflow accordingly. You can also find typical interruptions and distractions by tracking your time and creating management plans for them.

2. How to Put Time Tracking Into Practice

Time tracking can be implemented in a few different ways:

• Software for keeping track of time: Keep track of time spent on each task using tools like Harvest, RescueTime, or Toggl.

• Time logs: Assign each team member to manually record the time spent on a task.

• Clock in/clock out: To keep track of the amount of time spent on each project, put a clock in/clock out system in place.

Selecting a time-tracking technique that suits your team and workflow well is crucial.

3. Utilizing Time Tracking Information

After time tracking is implemented, utilizing the data to enhance team performance is crucial. Utilizing time tracking data in the following ways:

- Find areas for improvement: Analyze the time monitoring data to spot trends that indicate areas where your team is overspending or where efficiency may be increased.
- Establish objectives: Set objectives for your team using time monitoring data, such as reducing time spent on

particular tasks or raising output levels overall.

• Assess team performance: Utilize time-tracking information to assess each team member's work and pinpoint areas where they can benefit from more guidance or instruction.

• Raise the accuracy of project estimates: To enhance project estimates and guarantee that upcoming projects are finished on schedule and under budget, use time monitoring data.

Actual Cases

Here are a few actual instances of time monitoring being applied to enhance team performance:

• To determine which jobs use the most time, a marketing agency employs time-tracking software and modifies their workflow accordingly. Additionally, they use time-tracking data to pinpoint frequent distractions and create management plans for them.

• A software development company uses a clock-in/clock-out system to monitor the time spent on each project. They set goals for their staff and use the data to pinpoint areas where productivity may be increased.

• Members of a graphic design team maintain a handwritten record of the amount of time spent on each work. They assess each team member's performance using the data, and if necessary, they offer more assistance or training.

Final Thoughts

Time tracking and reporting are essential to managing a productive team. Maintaining track of the time spent on each task allows you to set objectives and improve project estimations. After determining which time-tracking method is most effective for your group, apply the data to boost output. Remember to remind your employees of the importance of time monitoring and to inspire them to do it correctly and often.

Practice: Time Monitoring

- Select a project or set of tasks presently being worked on by your team and related to a certain goal.

- Establish a completion date for the assignment. This goal should be realistic and achievable, given the skills of your team and the resources at your disposal.
- Assign your employees to log their time on each assignment using a spreadsheet or time-tracking software. Ask them to log how much time they spend on each task or subtask as part of the larger project.
- Examine the time monitoring data regularly, ideally once or twice weekly. Examine trends in the time allotted to each task or subtask to identify areas where your staff might be working too hard or too little.

- Using the time monitoring data, adjust the workflow for your team as needed. For example, you may consider providing additional training or resources to a team member who consistently puts in more time than the others on a particular task to help them become more productive.
- Record the time you spend on the task until it is completed. Compare the time you spent with the goal you set to improve going forward.

Measuring the amount of time spent on a given task or project can reveal a lot about your team's productivity and identify opportunities for improvement. By using this exercise to maximize team performance, you may be able to meet company objectives more quickly and efficiently.

How Well Do You Manage Your Time in Chapter 4?

Despite our best efforts, it appears to be something we cannot get away from. Time management seems to be something we should all be concerned about and working to become experts at, given the countless conversations surrounding it, the books on the subject, and the seminars on the subject. However, I have a serious issue with this strategy and its false sense of time management.

Two common fallacies that the majority of us are guilty of holding are the root cause of this issue:

1. You are genuinely capable of managing your time.
2. Effective time management is essential to achieving your goals.

Let us examine No. 1: You can learn to manage your time. Whether we like it or not, we are powerless over time. We are unable to accelerate. It cannot be slowed down. Some of it cannot be put away until later. There's nothing we can do about time, no matter how much work and effort we put into trying to control it. Furthermore, it wouldn't matter even if we could control time.

Changing the Perspective

As an entrepreneur, the outcome is what truly matters to me and, I suppose, most of you. Furthermore, a result is not a time-based output. It doesn't always follow that an essay I spend four hours writing is superior to one I simply spend an hour on. A one-hour piece can occasionally be far superior to a four-hour piece.

Thus, a great deal of effort is being expended by the majority of us in an attempt to manage something inconsequential and impossible for us to manage. But what other option is there? Recall the one-hour piece that was more successful than the four-hour one. Why?

All of it boils down to a topic we don't discuss nearly enough: focus. Certainly, an hour of intense concentration can yield better results than four hours of disinterested work. Put another way; our output is more a function of our focus on the task than the amount of time we spend on it. This implies that we want to always strive for focus management instead of time management.

Just review the two false beliefs I mentioned earlier regarding time management. If you replace the word "focus" with "time," you'll see that they change from untrue to true.

You can control how you focus.

2. One key to achieving outcomes is learning to manage your focus.

By embracing your task focus, getting more done in less time also helps you feel more productive and less overwhelmed (and may even help you obtain more vacation time!).

How to Practice Attention Management

Improving your focus overall by doing "in the zone" work and focus training, along with implementing that mentality into your day-to-day planning, is what it means to work on your focus management.

Here are some helpful hints, methods, and links:

1. Develop your ability to concentrate.

It's true that concentration functions like a muscle and that it may be developed. This should be your first action unless you already possess extraordinary concentration abilities.

2. Give up attempting to squeeze in extra time or work more quickly.

Not only is it extremely stressful to be rushing to get things done, but it also makes it unlikely that you will produce high-quality work. It will be simpler for you to produce more impactful outcomes if you embrace the fact that you cannot locate extra time and instead focus on how much attention you spend on a task. An alternative perspective is to strive for efficacy (a principle of attention management) rather than efficiency (a scheduling principle).

3. Make an effort to focus within the parameters of your schedule.

Plan more than simply the time needed to do each job on your to-do list or timetable. Rather, schedule a time to dedicate all your attention to the subject at hand. For instance, set aside 30 minutes to write without interruptions, turn off your electronics and notifications, and unplug from the internet. This is one of my favorite uses for timers.

4. Decide when you work best.

Finding the attention and complete engagement necessary for a task is frequently easier said than done. Your brain simply doesn't feel like working together sometimes. How can you counter this? Determine when you work best. Determining what time of day you typically perform best for particular jobs will help you identify your prime hour.

For instance, I've discovered that while social chores are better for me in the afternoon, creative jobs are more natural and can be completed more successfully in the morning. I've therefore made every effort to modify my timetable to account for this.

I want you to keep in mind the following four points from this chapter:

1. It is impossible for you to truly manage your time.

2. You are genuinely capable of controlling your attention.

3. Time management is not a crucial skill for achieving success.

4. One key to achieving outcomes is learning to manage your focus.

Go ahead and schedule some concentrated work now!

Chapter 17: Strategies for Delegation

An essential ability for any manager or business owner is delegation. Giving up control and trusting others to finish work for you might be difficult, but it's necessary to free up time and concentrate on the most important parts of your business. In this chapter, we will look at a few delegation strategies that will assist you in assigning duties to others and efficiently managing your workload.

Describe the assignment: Clearly defining a task before assigning it is essential. Make sure the individual you are delegating knows exactly what is expected of them and the desired outcome. By doing this, you can be confident.

Select the appropriate individual: The suitable individual must be chosen for the assignment before it can be delegated. Look for someone with the expertise and experience to finish the job well. Ensure the person has the time to do the assignment without getting overwhelmed by their workload.

Establish due dates: Establishing due dates for assigned work might help guarantee that it gets done on schedule. It also gives everyone a sense of urgency and keeps them on course. Ensure the individual you assign the work to is aware of the deadline and has adequate time to finish it.

Assist: Offering assistance and direction when assigning a task is critical. This can involve offering materials or responding to inquiries to support the individual in finishing the activity effectively. Making sure the task is moving along according to plan can also be ensured via routine check-ins.

Provide feedback: After finishing the task, let the person who finished it know what you thought. This might involve compliments as well as recommendations for development. Giving someone feedback can aid in their skill development and future work improvement.

The realm of sports is a great illustration of efficient delegation. Successful coaches assign assignments to their players and assistant coaches to ensure everything goes as planned. For instance, an offensive coordinator might be responsible for creating the team's playbook by a football coach. This frees the coach to concentrate on team-related duties like player development and game planning.

In the business sector, businesses looking to expand and thrive, like Amazon, have also adopted delegation. Jeff Bezos, founder of Amazon, is renowned for giving his executives more responsibility and authority to make decisions, freeing him up to concentrate on the company's overarching strategy and vision. Amazon has grown to be part of this delegation.

To sum up, delegation is an effective strategy that managers and business owners may use to free up time and concentrate on the most important facets of their jobs. You may effectively delegate and guarantee that tasks are completed by providing clear instructions, selecting the best candidate for the position, establishing deadlines, offering assistance, and providing feedback. Recall that time is money; therefore, you may reclaim your time and concentrate on what matters by assigning duties to others.

Successful Guidance

Being a leader is a crucial ability for company owners and entrepreneurs. Setting clear goals, motivating and directing your team toward a common vision, and giving them the tools and encouragement required to reach those goals are all components of effective leadership. We will examine the phases of successful leadership in this chapter and offer advice and anecdotes to help you improve as a leader.

Phase 1: Introspection

The foundation of effective leadership is self-awareness. You must know your values, strengths, and shortcomings to successfully lead your team. Cause them to be oblivious to their shortcomings, which lowers team morale and decreases output.

Regularly asking your team for input is one approach to becoming more self-aware. Seek their candid feedback on your communication, decision-making, and leadership style. Consider their criticism positively and focus on strengthening your areas of weakness.

Step 2: Forming a solid team

Creating a solid team is the second step in becoming a good leader. Talented people who share your vision and strive towards shared objectives must be drawn to and retained by you.

Making your company culture appealing is one approach to draw in talented people. The greatest candidates are typically drawn to organizations prioritizing employee engagement, growth potential, and work-life balance. Remember that time is money, and you want to draw in people who can work well and share your beliefs.

Give your team members regular feedback, chances for professional development, and acknowledgment of their achievements if you want them to stay on the team. Let them know you appreciate their contributions and are concerned about their well-being.

Step 3: Skillful dialogue

It takes effective communication to be a successful leader. Your team members must understand your vision, objectives, and expectations. Additionally, you must actively hear their opinions and concerns.

Regular team meetings, individual sessions with team members, and performance evaluations can all help to enhance communication. You can discuss problems or concerns, make goals, and offer feedback during these meetings.

Step 4: Giving your staff more authority

Giving your team the tools, encouragement, and freedom they require to succeed entails empowering them. You must provide duties to your team members and have faith in them. In order to save time and reclaim time to concentrate on other critical facets of your organization, delegation is essential.

Giving your team members the education and resources they require to perform their jobs well is one method to empower them. Give them the freedom to take responsibility for their work while offering assistance and support when required.

Step 5: Setting a good example

Set an example for others to follow. Inspiration since your deeds speak louder than words. Demonstrate your willingness to work personally if you want your teammates to work hard.

Establishing and pursuing specific goals is one approach to lead by example. Regularly update your teammates on your progress and share your team's successes.

To sum up, the key components of a good leadership style are self-awareness, team building, communication, empowerment, and setting an example for others. Remember that time is money, and to succeed as a leader, you must make the most of your time. You may improve as a leader and guide your team to success by adhering to these phases and pointers.

Chapter 1: Almost There

Imagine living in a future where long commutes are a thing of the past, work-life balance is achievable, and professional advancement is unrestricted by physical location. With remote employment becoming increasingly common, many people's dreams are coming true.

A McKinsey report from 2022 emphasizes this change: Of the

respondents, 23% can work remotely one to four days a week, and 35% can work from home full-time. Of the employed respondents, 41% did not have the option to work remotely at all, and just 13% could work remotely at least part of the time but decided not to (McKinsey & Company, 2022).

After reading these figures, you can realize how many professionals' lives are affected by remote work. How we approach our careers and live our lives is changing due to remote employment. However, how does this affect you as a team leader working remotely?

"We need to take a more flexible approach to both the workplace and the work we do—one, says David Coplin,

Chief Envisioning Officer at Microsoft UK (Agency, 2020). Coplin provides insightful advice.

In order to realize the advantages of remote work, Coplin stresses the significance of adjusting to new working practices. Many issues that workers have experienced since the dawn of the working world have been resolved by remote employment, including long commutes, difficulties juggling work and family obligations, and constraints on one's ability to advance personally and professionally.

The advantages of managing remote teams surpass the first discomfort, even though the shift from regular office environments may initially appear frightening. Workers who accept working remotely discover strategies to reduce distractions, boost output, and enhance their general well-being. The rise of remote labor in the business sector was unavoidable and was spurred by social and economic needs rather than created by them.

It is entirely up to you as a leader in remote team management to lead your team to success in this new environment. The reasons for remote work and the tactics to support you and your team in thriving in a remote work environment are covered in the following sections.

Accepting the Advantages of Remote Work: The Effect on Individuals, Groups, and Businesses

The shift to remote work poses issues for management as well as staff. Nevertheless, there are substantial advantages to these difficulties that greatly exceed the initial discomfort. Success and expansion in the ever-evolving company environment driven by social and economic pressures require adapting to remote work.

While some people may find the transition to remote work challenging, we must consider the total impact on productivity and acknowledge that the benefits outweigh the early challenges.

We can all benefit from a more productive and peaceful workplace if we welcome change and adjust to new working practices.

We've already seen how age and background barriers are broken down by technology and smartphones, which have become essential to our everyday lives. With remote work, we can keep pushing the envelope of what's feasible in the business world.

It doesn't have to be difficult to work remotely. We can make employment easier to manage, inexpensive, and accessible by utilizing technology improvements. Let's examine a few benefits of working remotely for small and large companies (VirtualVocations, 2021).

The benefits include lower costs for both businesses and employees. Since remote work does not require office space, firms can save money on utilities and rent. Workers save money on their commutes, and the economy and the company's carbon footprint benefit from the lessened environmental effect.

Less Equipment Needed: Employees can communicate with management and other staff members using their PCs or laptops, negating the need for extra equipment. Businesses can supply the Equipment if required.

Better Communication Channels: Unlike looking for coworkers in a real office, virtual workspaces like Slack facilitate more effective communication among team members.

Decreased Chaos: Working remotely makes collaborating easier and keeps things professional during online sessions. Employee stress also decreases because they don't have to worry about outside influences interfering with their work, such as traffic or personal emergencies. More contented workers are more productive and less easily distracted.

Flexibility to Work from Anywhere: Employees who work remotely are not bound by the daily commute and can work from their living room, a local café, or any other location.

Because of this flexibility, employees can work for organizations anywhere in the world and can avoid the hassle of moving closer to the office. Employees can now choose their employers and working conditions with more freedom.

The Power of Choice: Independent contractors can choose between working a regular 8-hour shift and a more flexible 2-hour daily commitment. Getting the intended outcomes in before the deadline is crucial.

Diverse Opportunities: Working remotely allows staff members to pursue various interests and career goals. Remote workers can create a more rewarding career path and diversify their experiences by working for different companies.

Although working remotely has many advantages, it's important to be aware of and prepare for any potential difficulties. Chapter 1 explains the meaning of productivity and time management and explains their importance.

This chapter will teach you ● What time management and productivity are and how they connect.

● The advantages of enhancing your productivity and time management abilities.

● The prevalent fallacies and misunderstandings around productivity, time management, and solutions.

Time management: What is it?

The deliberate practice of appropriately organizing and arranging your tasks is known as time management. It's a technique used to deliberately manage how much time is spent on various tasks, primarily to boost output, effectiveness, and efficiency.

Time management aims not to accomplish more tasks in less time. It all comes down to acting appropriately when necessary. It involves setting priorities for your projects based on their urgency and importance and scheduling your time appropriately. It also involves being able to adjust and change with the times, as well as handle disruptions and divert attention.

What Does Productivity Mean?

Put another way, it refers to how much you accomplish with the time, energy, money, talents, and other resources at your disposal. Various contexts, including business, education, the home, health, and hobbies, might benefit from productivity.

It is not productive to work longer or harder. Working better and more intelligently is the goal. It involves figuring out how to decrease the cost and waste of your input while increasing the amount and quality of your output. It also involves connecting your work to your values and ambitions and discovering its fulfillment and meaning.

How do productivity and time management relate to each other?

Productivity and time management are closely related ideas. Both of them want to enable you to accomplish more with less. Planning, arranging, setting priorities, carrying out, keeping an eye on, and assessing your work are all necessary for both. Both rely on your capacity for awareness, planning, and adaptation.

Productivity and time management are two different things, though. Even if you have excellent time management skills, your work may still be of poor quality or irrelevant. On the other hand, even if you excel at generating worthwhile or high-quality work, you could still squander a lot of time or miss deadlines. To get the best outcomes, you must so balance the two factors.

Why Are Productivity and Time Management Important?

Increasing your productivity and time management abilities will benefit you greatly in many aspects of your life. Among these advantages are:

Increased productivity and efficiency: You can do more tasks quickly and with fewer resources and effort. Additionally, you can raise the standard and worth of your output.

● Less stress: You can lessen the strain and anxiety brought on by expectations, workload, deadlines, and interruptions.

Procrastination, feeling overwhelmed, and exhaustion can also be avoided.

● A stronger reputation in the workplace: Your dependability and performance might win over your supervisor, associates, clients, or customers

● More opportunities: You can make more room for fresh endeavors, difficulties, or educational chances. It's also possible to discover new passions or interests.

● Greater fulfillment and balance: You can attain greater harmony in your personal and professional lives. You can also relish having extra time for your priorities or yourself.

Frequently Held Myths and Misconceptions Regarding Productivity and Time Management

While productivity and time management are important, many people have misconceptions that keep them from enhancing their performance or general well-being. The following are some widespread misunderstandings and fallacies around productivity and time management:

Myth 1: Effective time management entails adhering to a strict timetable or regimen.

Effective time management involves being adaptive and flexible in various circumstances. Routines and schedules help you better organize your time; they shouldn't stifle your imagination or prevent you from being spontaneous.

- Myth 2: Being productive means multitasking or doing everything oneself.

Reality: Being productive is about putting your finest effort or most important tasks to use. Occasionally, this entails assigning or contracting out certain work to more qualified or efficient people. It also entails concentrating on a single task instead of attempting to multitask.

Myth 3: Only those who are overly busy or workaholics can effectively manage their time.

Everyone who wants to maximize their time should learn time management skills. Regardless of how much or little work you have, improving your time management will always be beneficial. Effective time management does not entail scheduling activities for every minute of the day; it involves making deliberate and prudent time management decisions. Additionally, time management is about striking a healthy balance between work and play rather than working nonstop.

The Importance of Continuous Improvement

Time management has always been a major issue for humans, from the ancient Egyptian time hourglasses to the contemporary usage of apps and software to track and optimize every minute. Driven by the conviction that continuous development is essential to optimizing our effectiveness and efficiency, time management has developed and improved over time.

Constant improvement is a way of life, an unwavering dedication to development and personal progress. It goes beyond just doing tasks faster. By using this idea in our time management, we may lead more balanced, effective, and satisfying lives.

Continuous learning is necessary for time management to continually improve. To enhance our time management abilities, we must be willing to examine our routines and habits critically, pinpoint areas that need work, and make conscious decisions. The foundation of this approach is self-assessment, which is how we spend our time.

One common way to conceptualize continuous development is using the Japanese word "kaizen." In business, kaizen refers to initiatives involving every employee, from CEOs to assembly line workers, in continuously improving all operations and processes. Adopting a kaizen perspective on time management entails always seeking methods to optimize our time utilization.

The capacity to adapt and change with the times is an essential component of continuous progress in time management. Our lives are dynamic; our obligations and situations occasionally shift unanticipatedly. A time management technique that was successful in the past may be ineffective now. As a result, we need to be open to trying new tactics, making required adjustments to our plans, and being flexible with our routines and habits.

Furthermore, it's critical to remember that continuous improvement does not equate to instant perfection. There may be setbacks and slow progress at times. In these situations, it's critical to remember that continuous development is a process rather than a goal. Every small step towards our objective of better time management is encouraging, and every error or setback presents a chance for improvement.

Regularly enhancing our time management skills can also benefit other areas of our lives. It can enhance our mental well-being by lessening the tension and worry brought on by feeling overburdened and disorganized, enabling us to spend more time with them. It can increase our efficacy and productivity at work, resulting in more successful careers and employment prospects.

To put it briefly, perpetual improvement holds great potential to transform our lives and our ability to manage our time effectively. The rewards are great, but it takes commitment, introspection, and a readiness to change and advance. By starting this journey of continuous development, we empower ourselves, enhance our quality of life, and optimize how we use our time. Thus, let us not undervalue the significance of continuously enhancing our time management skills; they may hold the key to a richer and more satisfying life.

Chapter 8: Handling Time Constraints and Adjusting to Shifts

Determining the usual time limits Time restrictions are a common barrier that might impede effective time management. Among them include poor procedures, irrational expectations, procrastination, diversions, and lack of prioritization. Find out your specific time limitations and how they impact your ability to manage your time and be productive. Acknowledging these problems is the first step towards solving and resolving them.

Developing strategies to deal with procrastination Procrastination is a significant time hurdle for many people. Establish deadlines for every stage of the procedure. Use the Pomodoro Technique or time-blocking to create intervals of concentrated work and build momentum. Minimise disruptions and promote an efficient work environment. Develop a focused, disciplined mindset to finish tasks on schedule and avoid more delays.

Managing interruptions and maintaining focus Interruptions to workflow lower productivity. To prevent disturbances, set limitations, let coworkers know when you're available, and use the "do not disturb" feature on your devices. Practice effective communication to minimize unnecessary interruptions. You can create defined blocks of uninterrupted work time by setting aside time for certain tasks and informing others of your absence during those times. You can stay focused and get the most out of your work by controlling interruptions.

Adapting to novel circumstances and unanticipated incidents It is inevitable that change will occur, and effective time management demands the ability to adjust. Keep an open mind and be prepared to adjust your ideas if unanticipated events arise. Use your problem-solving skills and resilience to devise several plans of action when faced with challenges or adjustments. Learn from the past and seek growth opportunities. If you can adapt to change, you can better organize your schedule and handle uncertainty.

Constant development and learning Improving one's time management skills is a lifelong endeavor. Seek opportunities for personal and professional development to strengthen your time management skills. Tactics and approaches for optimizing productivity and using your time most. Choose the solutions that work best for you after considering your past experiences. As needed to improve efficiency and address issues.

Managing deadlines and adapting to changes requires a proactive and adaptable approach. By understanding how to deal with interruptions, embrace continuous learning, deal with procrastination, and respond to changes, you may better manage your time and handle time-related challenges.

The final few chapters will cover the techniques for developing a positive mindset, finding both professional and personal fulfillment, and maintaining long-term success in time management. Combining these ideas with skills and techniques for effective time management will help you live a successful, fulfilling, and balanced life.

1.5 Reevaluating and Modifying Your Objectives

Our priorities shift with the times, as do our lives. To make the most of your time and keep your attention on what is important, it is imperative that you periodically review and modify your priorities. To assist you in reevaluating and reordering your priorities, consider these steps:

1. Consider your objectives: Review your long- and short-term objectives regularly. Assess whether they still fit your goals, values, and situation. Modify your objectives if needed to better align them with your present priorities.

2. Assess your progress: Determine how well your present prioritization techniques work and how far you've come towards your goals. Determine any barriers or difficulties that impede your development and consider ways to overcome them.

3. Identify changes in your life: Think about if you've had any major life changes, including a new job, a shift in your family's situation, or taking on more duties. Your priorities might need to change as a result of these adjustments.

4. Reorder tasks: Using strategies like the Eisenhower Matrix or the ABCDE method, rearrange your tasks in order of importance based on your analysis and reflection. Your to-do list should be updated to reflect your changed priorities.

5. Assign or remove duties: You could discover that some chores can be assigned to others or are no longer

necessary when you reevaluate your priorities. Assign or do away with these duties to make more time for higher-priority work.

6. Modify your schedule: After reevaluating your priorities, you might need to change your timetable to accommodate new assignments or give high-priority activities more time. Ensure that your time blocks, calendar, and daily schedule all match your revised priorities.

7. Remain adaptable: Recognise that your priorities could shift over time, and be ready to make adjustments as necessary. It takes flexibility and adaptability to manage your time well and keep a good work-life balance.

Making the most of your time and focusing on what is important requires you to regularly review and revise your priorities. Time management techniques stay useful and consistent with your objectives and morals.

Recognising time wasters and put off tasks.

Effective time management starts with recognizing time wasters and procrastinating. Activities or practices that take up your time but don't add much value or benefit are called time-wasters. Conversely, procrastination is putting off or delaying obligations or tasks. These two have the potential to significantly reduce your productivity and keep you from reaching your objectives.

Consider, for instance, that you are a student with a significant exam approaching. You know you should study and prepare for the test, but you find yourself watching TV or browsing social media for hours instead of studying. Even though these pursuits may be entertaining, they don't offer much value or benefit and take up time that could be spent learning.

Similarly, picture yourself as a professional with a significant project deadline approaching. However, you find yourself putting off finishing the project instead of working on it. The project is approaching its deadline, but you haven't made any headway. You keep putting it off. This procrastination may result in a last-minute rush, which may result in lower-quality work or even miss the deadline.

Recognizing time wasters and procrastination is critical to being conscious of your everyday routine and activities. One way to get started would be to maintain a time journal to record your daily activities. This can help you discover the tasks that are taking up your time without adding much value and provide a clear picture of where your time is going.

Once the time wasters have been discovered, it's critical to devise strategies for their reduction or elimination. This could be putting time limitations on how much you watch TV or use social media, or it could entail finding more useful methods to use your free time. One way to combat procrastination is to divide difficult activities into smaller, more doable portions and establish self-imposed deadlines. Another option is to look for self-motivation methods, such as rewarding yourself when you finish a task or finding a companion who can serve as an accountability partner.

Understanding the root cause of procrastination is another useful tactic for dealing with it. A lack of drive could bring it on, the difficulty of the task, or a fear of failing. You can identify solutions for the underlying cause once you know it. If the issue is, however, a lack of drive, you can try to identify ways to make the work more engaging or fulfilling. If the assignment seems too big to handle at once, consider dividing it into smaller parts and tackling each separately. If your fear is of failing, you can also try changing the way you think about it by emphasizing your progress rather than the final result.

C. Prioritizing work and establishing goals

Prioritizing work and setting goals are two crucial components of efficient time management. While setting priorities helps you make the most use of your time by concentrating on the most critical things first, goals provide direction and concentration.

Consider, for instance, that you are a student who wishes to raise your GPA. A

4.0 GPA would be an objective for you. You must establish SMART goals—specific, measurable, realistic, relevant, and time-bound—in order to accomplish this aim. One could set specific goals like studying for three hours a day, measurable goals like scoring at least 90% on your next math test, achievable goals like hiring a tutor, relevant goals like concentrating on math classes, and time-bound goals like finishing this task by the end of the semester.

Setting priorities for your work is crucial once your goals have been established. Setting priorities for your work guarantees that you make the best use of your time and helps you concentrate on the most important activities first. One well-liked method for work prioritization.

Important and urgent jobs are in Quadrant 1. These urgent chores will significantly affect your goals and must be completed immediately. For instance, getting ready for a math test the following day.

Important but not urgent jobs are in quadrant two. These are the kinds of things that, while necessary to reach your objectives, do not require immediate attention. For instance, studying and making plans for a project will take time.

Important yet urgent jobs are in quadrant three. These are urgent chores that won't significantly advance your objectives. For instance, responding to a friend's email.

Tasks in the fourth quadrant are not critical or urgent. These kinds of jobs can wait or be assigned and have little bearing on your objectives. For instance, leisurely online browsing.

You may make sure that you are spending your time on the most critical things first and not wasting it on low-priority chores by setting priorities for your tasks.

Adaptability and flexibility are crucial in prioritizing activities and creating goals. As circumstances change, it's critical to have the flexibility to reevaluate your objectives and ambitions. For instance, you might need to change your study time or approach if your routine isn't working. Similarly, you could need to rearrange your list of priorities to give priority to a newly discovered urgent task.

In conclusion, two critical components of efficient time management are goal-setting and job prioritization. You can make sure that you are making the most of your time and moving closer to your goals by prioritizing activities using tools like the Eisenhower matrix and creating clear, measurable, achievable, relevant, and time-bound goals. It's also critical to be adaptive and flexible, modifying your objectives and goals as necessary.

Put Quality Before Quantity to Overcome Multitasking

Although multitasking could appear like a good strategy, it frequently reduces productivity and encourages procrastination. One task at a time encourages comprehensive work, breaking the procrastination and distraction cycle.

Myth concerning multitasking

The quality and efficiency of each task suffer when you multitask because you are dividing your attention and cognitive resources. Procrastination might result from the sense of productivity when you multitask without completing them to a high standard.

The Art of Focusing on a Single Task

The Act of giving your whole attention to one task at a time is known as single-tasking. You will produce better work and be less likely to put off tasks if you fully commit to them and minimize outside distractions.

Saying no and delegating: Protect your time

Understanding your boundaries and knowing when to delegate work or back out of commitments are essential skills for time management. Time management helps you avoid overloading yourself and makes room for important chores.

Delegation authority

Assign work that can be done well by others. Allowing people to demonstrate their abilities allows you more time to engage in other activities. This strategy reduces overwork-related procrastination and avoids burnout.

The skill of refusing

Managing your time well requires avoiding extra obligations that don't fit your priorities. You can devote more of your time to the things that matter by politely dismissing assignments or initiatives that divert you.

Think, then Act Again: Maintain a Continuously Better Approach.

Efficient time management necessitates continuous introspection and adjustment. You can strengthen your resistance to procrastination by routinely assessing your tactics, recognizing areas for improvement, and making the required improvements.

Assessment and introspection

Review your development regularly to spot trends in your achievements and obstacles. Think about the effective tactics and those that require development.

ongoing education

Remain receptive to novel approaches and theories in time management. Seek possibilities to acquire and apply strategies that suit your objectives and demands.

In brief

Overcoming procrastination and taming the time thief demands a complex strategy based on efficient time management. You may maximize your time use and reduce delay cycles by using awareness, matching your actions to your beliefs, and utilizing time-saving strategies like the Pomodoro Technique and the Eisenhower Matrix. By consciously developing productive habits, mastery over your focus, and managing your time, you can design a full, balanced, and purposeful life. By incorporating these time management strategies into your everyday routine, you'll be able to overcome your procrastinating tendencies and take proactive steps toward your goals and personal development. Provide sophisticated techniques and perspectives to hone your strategy and effectively overcome procrastination.

Beyond the Pill: Using Medication and Therapy Together for Efficient Time Management)

A neurodevelopmental illness called ADHD affects a large number of people, including adults and children. It causes various issues, from difficulties finishing work and meeting deadlines to difficulties preserving relationships and adhering to social duties.

Thankfully, there are efficient ADHD treatments available to help patients control their symptoms and enhance their quality of life. The two most popular methods are medicine and counseling. Many experts concur that the best course of action for time management may involve a combination of medication and treatment, even if each might be beneficial.

The well-known psychologist Dr. Russell Barkley once remarked, "ADHD is not a problem of knowing what to do; it is a problem of doing what you know." This statement perfectly sums up the difficulty that individuals with ADHD have managing their time. They could find it difficult to consistently put their time management techniques and tools into practice, even if they do have them.

This chapter will examine how individuals with ADHD can overcome this obstacle with the help of both medication and therapy. We will go over the advantages and drawbacks of ADHD medication, the various forms of therapy that can help with time management, and the significance of an individualized treatment plan that incorporates both therapy and medicine.

Therapy based on cognitive behavior (CBT)

Individuals with ADHD frequently deal with certain issues that affect their day-to-day functioning, such as issues with organizing their schedules, being impulsive, controlling their emotions, and maintaining their self-worth. These difficulties may seriously affect their relationships, classroom or work performance, mental health, and wellbeing. It's critical to look for support and assistance from experts who are knowledgeable about this illness's nuances and can offer direction and resources for successfully managing its symptoms.

One such psychotherapy that allows you to take charge of your thoughts, feelings, and behaviors is cognitive behavioral therapy (CBT) (Padesky& Mooney, 2012). Positive patterns can take the place of negative ones to help you overcome emotional issues like sadness and anxiety and lead a better, more satisfying life.

Not only that, but cognitive behavioral therapy (CBT) can alter your life if you have ADHD and struggle with time management, organization, and stress reduction. With CBT, you'll learn useful skills like managing timers and planners, practicing relaxation techniques, and breaking down activities into manageable milestones.

However, CBT is not a one-size-fits-all method, so it's crucial to collaborate with a qualified therapist on your particular requirements. The therapy is a time-limited program usually consists of 12 to 20 sessions. It is structured and goal-oriented, giving clients the skills and tools to control their thoughts and behaviors.

Practice using the ABC Model

The ABC Model is one cognitive behavioral therapy (CBT) exercise type. The goal of this exercise is to assist people in recognizing the ideas, feelings, and actions that are causing them problems. Although it can be used to treat a variety of mental health issues, it is frequently used to treat depression and anxiety.

There are three steps in the ABC Model: A, B, and C. The letter "A" represents the Activating event or circumstance that sets off unfavorable feelings and ideas. "B" represents the individual's beliefs or views regarding the circumstance. These ideas influence an individual's emotional response and can be beneficial or detrimental. Lastly, "C" stands for the actions or consequences that follow from the feelings and ideas.

As an illustration, suppose someone struggling with social anxiety is invited to a party. The party invitation is the activating event. They may have negative views about the circumstance, such as "I won't know anyone there," "People will judge me," or "I'll make a fool of myself." The result of these negative thoughts is concern, anxiety, and anxiousness. After that, the person can decide not to attend the party.

The unfavorable ideas that are fueling their anxiety and helping them swap them out for more grounded, upbeat thoughts by employing the ABC Model exercise. The individual may learn to reframe their ideas to something like "It's okay to make mistakes," "People are usually friendly and welcoming," or "I might meet new people and have a good time." Positive feelings and actions, like going to the party, having fun, and making new friends, can result from this new set of beliefs.

A person having a panic attack while driving could be another instance of the ABC Model in action. Driving is the activating event, but the feeling that one would lose control and crash could cause panic and dread. The result could be that they drive less or never at all, which would greatly influence their day-to-day activities.

The individual can develop coping mechanisms to control their panic attacks while driving and question their negative mindset with the assistance of a therapist. They can lessen their worry and anxiety when driving by reframing their ideas to something like, "I've driven before without an accident," or "I can take steps to calm myself if I start to panic."

The ABC model is one CBT activity that might assist people in recognizing and challenging negative thoughts and actions.

Practice: Traveling Through Time

This is a creative and entertaining CBT activity to help you improve your time management abilities. To play, put yourself in the future and pretend you are looking back on your life. Consider this:

● By the you pass away, what do you hope to have accomplished?

● For what reason do you want to be remembered?

What actions are necessary for you to accomplish these objectives?

After determining your long-term objectives, divide them into more achievable, smaller phases. Consider this:

● How can you make progress toward your objectives today?

● How can you make better use of the time you have? Which duties can you assign or get rid of to make additional time?

You may improve your time management skills and have a stronger sense of purpose and direction by approaching your goals in this manner. It's beneficial to monitor your development and acknowledge your accomplishments. Time management is continuous, and practice is necessary to build these abilities. You can learn to accomplish your goals and manage your time more efficiently using CBT strategies.

Take regular breaks or use a standing desk to counteract the harmful effects of sitting.

Sedentary conduct has increased due to the long hours spent sitting at a desk in modern jobs. Sedentary activity has been linked in several studies to type 2 diabetes. Long periods of sitting can also have a detrimental effect on productivity and mental health. Because of their potential to lessen these harmful consequences, techniques like using a standing desk and taking frequent breaks have gained popularity.

A standing desk is a type of desk that enables comfortable standing work. It is sometimes referred to as a stand-up or height-adjustable desk. It promotes mobility and breaks up prolonged periods of sitting. By shifting from sitting to standing, you can activate different muscle groups, enhance circulation, and lessen the potential strain that extended sitting might put on your back. Furthermore, standing while working can help burn a few extra calories compared to sitting.

Standing desks have advantages, but it's crucial to remember that they won't reverse the harmful consequences of extended sitting on one's health. They should be applied in concert with a more comprehensive plan to promote activity and reduce sedentary behavior. This is because prolonged standing can also create weariness and discomfort. As a result, a balanced strategy known as sit-stand-switch is advised. This frequently shifts from a seated to a standing posture and back.

However, another useful tactic to counteract the detrimental effects of sitting is to take numerous breaks during the day. Often called "movement breaks" or "active breaks," these interludes comprise brief bursts of physical exertion, such as walking, stretching, or just getting up and moving around.

According to research, regularly taking breaks from sitting has been linked to several advantages. These include a lower chance of developing chronic illnesses, happier feelings, less weariness, and increased focus and productivity. Taking active breaks might also help you reach the daily physical activity recommendations.

The following tactics should be taken into consideration if you want to include frequent pauses in your daily routine:

1. Set Reminders: Make the most of technology by using your computer or phone to remind you to get up and move around every thirty minutes.

2. Put the Pomodoro Technique to Use.

3. Walk and Talk: If possible, take calls while strolling around, or even have meetings while strolling.

4. Stretch: Easy stretches you may perform anywhere will help ease tired and tense muscles.

In conclusion, taking regular rests and utilizing a standing desk can be useful tactics to lessen the harmful effects of extended sitting. They can encourage physical activity, enhance health outcomes, and even increase output. It's crucial to remember that these tactics should only be employed as a component of a well-rounded strategy for workplace wellbeing, which may also involve consistent physical activity, a balanced diet, and appropriate mental health procedures.

Make self-care a priority, incorporating rest, physical activity, and a balanced diet.

In today's world, where life and work frequently overlap, self-care might occasionally be neglected. However, it's essential to preserving both mental and physical health, and it directly impacts output. Making self-care a priority entails taking care of the body and mind via rest, physical activity, and a balanced diet—all of which improve general wellbeing and, consequently, performance and productivity.

First, sleep is a basic human requirement that immediately impacts physical and mental wellbeing. Many brain functions, such as cognition, concentration, productivity, and performance, depend on getting enough sleep. On the other hand, lack of sleep can harm these domains, causing deficiencies in creativity, attention, and decision-making—all of which are essential for efficiency. Thus, it's crucial to make sure you receive enough good sleep. A peaceful sleeping environment, minimizing screen time before bed, and staying away from coffee and large meals just before bed are all strategies to enhance sleep hygiene.

The next crucial component of self-care is exercise. Frequent exercise has several advantages, such as better mood, stress reduction, weight management, and cardiovascular health. Exercise can also increase memory and thinking abilities, stimulate creativity and productivity, and improve cognitive function. Even short bursts of exercise can provide instant advantages, including heightened energy and concentration. You don't have to spend hours at the gym to include exercise in your regimen. It may be as easy as going for a little stroll during lunch, doing some yoga in the morning, or working out quickly at home. Selecting enjoyable activities will increase the likelihood.

Finally, maintaining a balanced diet is essential to self-care. Our bodies and minds are fueled by our food, which impacts our mood, energy levels, and cognitive abilities. Meats and whole grains can supply the nutrients for the best possible brain performance. Staying hydrated is crucial because even a small amount of dehydration can affect mood, memory, and focus. Conversely, overindulging in processed foods, sugary snacks, and caffeinated beverages can impair mental clarity and cause energy collapses.

In addition to these external facets of self-care, mental and emotional components must also be considered. Examples include stress management, mindfulness training, social connection maintenance, and participation in enjoyable activities. These can support resilience development, uphold an optimistic outlook, and avert burnout.

Self-care—which includes getting enough sleep, exercising, and maintaining a good diet—is essential to productivity. Although it may appear that time spent on self-care equates to time away from the office, the truth is that we may improve our productivity and performance by attending to our physical and mental health. We can approach our work with our best selves—full of vigor, concentration, and optimism. Better results follow from this, and it also helps create a more fulfilling and sustainable way of living and working.

Irregular timing leads to tension.

Delaying things might cause tension. Your thoughts won't be clear if you try to concentrate on anything and keep putting it off. You'll take longer to complete tasks, which will eventually cause you to become more stressed. The longer this cycle goes on, the more difficult it is for your brain to get out of its rut and begin functioning normally.

Procrastination-related stress is bad for your health as well. Stress has been connected to several illnesses, including diabetes and heart disease, but it can also aggravate other bodily issues, such as headaches or stomachaches, by gradually lowering immunity.

With all these bad feelings, you can even be nervous about starting your task! Nothing is worse than being aware that crucial tasks need to be completed but being overcome with panic every time those tasks aren't completed immediately or at all. This makes sense when we consider how our brains are wired: they are made to help us feel good when we do things we enjoy (like watching TV), but not so much when we do things that aren't enjoyable but still require our attention (like doing the dishes). This is one of the reasons why some people find it more difficult than others to overcome their procrastinating tendencies; they could find themselves torn between two equally unpleasant options: either putting up with their obligations while feeling miserable about them OR ignoring them completely and feeling bad about it later on when they have to face the consequences of their decisions because of what went wrong the last time.

Both talent and time are wasted.

Furthermore, it's a waste of talent as well as assets. And cash. as well as potential. And opportunity; even if you're unaware of it, you're probably wasting all these things daily! We deliberately choose not to use our strengths and abilities for something that matters to us and the people around us when we put off accomplishing the things we need or want to get done. By putting off what needs to be done until later (or never), we can choose not to have an influence or to give away our talents.

This is the reason procrastination is so unpleasant. By using avoidance and delay strategies, we not only let ourselves miss out on what could be but also waste our potential as people, robbing others of our gifts!

When you put things off, you feel bad and embarrassed.

A time thief is a procrastination. It robs you of priceless moments and makes you feel ashamed and terrible.

- You have negative self-esteem. You may feel like a failure if your procrastination results in missed deadlines or subpar work that is submitted. If this occurs often, you can even start to question your worth or ability.
- Being a procrastinator can make you feel untrustworthy. It doesn't imply someone doesn't exist just because they have never been made aware of their shortcomings! Sometimes, we are so afraid of rejection that we hide behind our masks rather than take the chance of being rejected. But if we do this for a long enough period, eventually, those masks become who we are, and nobody

will be able to identify the true "us" underneath them (assuming there was ever a "us" at all).

Your life will become chaotic if you put things off.

The primary issue is that there will be a lot on your plate, making it difficult to remember everything that has to be done. Your life becomes chaotic as a result. Your mind will be racing with so many things that you won't be able to finish anything, and you'll be anxious about everything on your list that you haven't yet crossed off.

Furthermore, delaying tasks can make it more difficult for us to concentrate on them when we eventually try to finish them. Our culture has constantly conditioned us to be preoccupied with incoming messages and notifications. However, they can become a habit if we don't respond to them immediately.

A person who procrastinates loses self-esteem.

If your procrastination becomes a chronic issue, you'll experience guilt and humiliation. You'll lose out on enjoyable chances and time spent on tasks you detest, like housework or other chores. Your ability to break free from the unpleasant emotions linked to procrastination will become more difficult as this cycle of guilt, shame, and procrastination repeats.

The more time that goes by while you're not accomplishing something significant, the longer you put off doing something unpleasant. After a while, it will be too late to achieve those objectives if this continues!

If you put things off for too long, you'll miss out on enjoyable experiences.

You enjoy, which is one of the best things about living in the modern world. You can paint, draw, skateboard, swim, volunteer at a soup kitchen, etc. The possibilities are endless. However, if you wait until tomorrow when you'll have more time and energy to complete these tasks, they might never be done.

If you wait to start learning how to play an instrument until later, when your schedule finally opens up (which it never does), then your window of chance to take music lessons has gone! The exciting decision to start piano lessons will now have to wait another year as it got buried under all the other "more important" commitments, such as job and family duties.

Perhaps you were asked out for coffee once, but you decided against accepting the invitation straight away because it looked like fun at the time. However, months have passed, and now there's a new chance that looks even more exciting than going out for coffee with the original person.

If you put off doing anything now, it will become worse later!

Procrastination is a habit, as you can see. Writers know that habits are difficult to break and will only worsen if left unchecked. Your habits will get worse down the road if you don't make the necessary changes today. Procrastination grows larger and larger with time, much like a snowball. The harder it is to complete a delayed assignment or activity, the longer you wait to begin working on it!

What benefits can time management offer?

There are basic advantages to time management. You can accomplish more in less time, giving you more time for yourself, improving your ability to concentrate, increasing your productivity, reducing stress, and spending more time with the people you care about.

When you manage your time well, reaching larger goals and ambitions is simpler and more effective. In addition to increasing productivity and efficiency, time management reduces stress. You may work less and generate more with good time management skills.

Efficient time management enhances both productivity and concentration. They also reduce distractions and procrastination. Effective time management boosts efficiency. It also allows you to accomplish your important tasks more swiftly and efficiently.

Ten benefits of time management are listed below.

1. Decreased stress

Making time for organization reduces stress and increases self-assurance. Additionally, time management reduces worry and stress. Establishing and adhering to deadlines is essential for efficient time management.

If you manage your time well, you can prevent yourself from constantly feeling exhausted and under pressure. If you are adept at managing your time, you can better use your available time. Productivity increases when you can do the most important things. When there is less stress, you are more confident and clear about how to spend your time.

Reducing stress improves performance and improves sleep. It also encourages a more favorable work-life balance.

Identify three sources of strain that are interfering with your time management skills. Investigate the root causes of your stress and the potential outcomes of removing it. Choose one action you can do to eliminate the biggest source of stress. 2. A better work-life balance

A good work-life balance is one of the main benefits of time management. Achieving a better work-life balance will increase your productivity at work and free up more time for the people in your life that matter most.

Work-life balance creates harmony between an individual's personal and professional lives. You run the danger of burnout and chronic fatigue when you work long hours.

3. Greater flexibility in leisure time

Time liberation is one of the primary advantages of time management. Setting and accomplishing your most important goals could take precedence when you have more free time.

You might spend more time with your loved ones since you have more time for yourself. There is more time available to form new connections and pursue interests. You can fulfill your mission if you have more free time and flexibility.

Consider your weekly schedule if you have an additional five or ten hours of spare time. Make a list of your top three priorities and consider the impact on your life if you implemented them. Next, create a simple action plan to help you implement these adjustments.

4. A stronger focus

Time management that works will improve your productivity and focus. Focusing more intently will help you seize greater opportunities. It also allows you to dedicate more time to the things, people, and objectives that truly matter to you.

Time management is essential for better attention and prioritizing. You become more focused and in control of your day as you improve at managing your time.

Extending working hours and taking on additional tasks are not instances of proficient time management. When it comes to time management, work smarter, not harder.

When you effectively manage your time, you may devote more attention to your most productive endeavors. This encourages virtuous behaviors. It also ensures that you devote more time to activities that help you reach your objectives.

5. Higher degrees of effectiveness

Effective time management strategies enable you to do more and be more productive.

Your time management abilities will determine how well you can set priorities and reduce stress. You may better manage your time by defining your objectives and establishing priorities for the most important things. You will, therefore, have more time to generate more and better outcomes.

Time management can help you organize your day and improve your performance. When you organize your days ahead, you become more productive. The majority of time management depends on time management. Efficiency and production are increased via planning.

To make better use of your time, you must establish daily priorities. Establishing priorities can help you focus your most productive time on finishing them.

6. Reduction in postponement

Procrastination is a direct result of poor time management. Procrastination is easy when your goals are unclear and hard to concentrate on. Distraction and procrastination are the outcomes of ineffective time management.

Learning efficient time management strategies and time management would help you prevent procrastination. Procrastination is avoided when you feel in charge of your responsibilities because of time management.

You're less prone to procrastinate when feeling productive and in charge of your schedule. Having well-defined goals allows you to focus more on the most crucial tasks.

Enumerate your top three reasons for procrastinating, then outline the first measures you can take to address each one personally.

7. Everything is straightforward and easier

Effective time management techniques simplify and expedite tasks. You feel more competent and confident when you are in charge of your schedule. You can spend your time more clearly and confidently when practicing effective time management. You no longer feel stressed, anxious, or frustrated as a result.

Effective time management allows you to fulfill your goals and create helpful to-do lists. This method makes it easier for you to prioritize your most important tasks. You invest the time and energy required to achieve the intended objectives and outcomes.

Find out which time-management techniques work best for establishing priorities.

8. Reduction in distraction

Effective time management increases focus and decreases distractions.

Distraction lowers time management abilities and impedes productivity.

Mastering time management skills reduces distractions and increases attention. Effective time management increases the success of your planning and prioritization processes. This facilitates the scheduling of your most crucial tasks.

Effective time managers allocate time blocks to the most critical tasks. They should also establish time limitations in order to improve their focus.

Better boundaries ensure more concentration and time spent on your primary goals. Additionally, it reduces stress and diverticula.